Who God says I am

GIRLS EDITION

WHO GOD SAYS I AM

© 2020 Michele Arnold. All rights reserved.

THE HOLY BIBLE, NEW INTERNATIONAL VERSION®, NIV® Copyright © 1973, 1978, 1984, 2011 by Biblica, Inc.® Used by permission. All rights reserved worldwide.

All rights reserved. No part of this publication may be reproduced, stored in a retrieval system or transmitted in any form or by any means, electronic, mechanical, photocopying, recording or otherwise without the prior permission of the publisher or in accordance with the provisions of the Copyright, Designs and Patents Act 1988 or under the terms of any licence permitting limited copying issued by the Copyright Licensing Agency.

Illustrations used with permission by contributor via canva

ISBN - 978-1-7351373-9-1

Published by In His Grace Ministries LLC

Book website: www.inhisgrace.com/product/who-god-says-i-am-girls-edition/

Dedication

To my little Poppy seed. You have stolen mmma's (grandma's) heart. I love you so very much! I want you to know and understand the LOVE that God has for you. I want for you to know who you are in Christ. He loves you so very much. His mercies are new every morning. His grace abounds and His heart overflows for you.

I am Chosen

"You did not choose me, but I chose you and appointed you so that you might go and bear fruit—fruit that will last—and so that whatever you ask in my name the Father will give you."
John 15:16

I am *Loved*

"And so we know and rely on the love God has for us. God is love. Whoever lives in love lives in God, and God in them."
1 John 4:16

I am *Valuable*

"Look at the birds of the air; they do not sow or reap or store away in barns, and yet your heavenly Father feeds them. Are you not much more valuable than they?"
Matthew 6:26

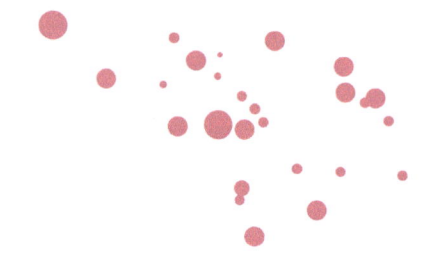

I am *Blessed*

"Praise be to the God and Father of our Lord Jesus Christ, who has blessed us in the heavenly realms with every spiritual blessing in Christ."
Ephesians 1:3

I am *Confident*

"Let us then approach God's throne of grace with confidence, so that we may receive mercy and find grace to help us in our time of need."
Hebrews 4:16

I am His *Friend*

"I no longer call you servants, because a servant does not know his master's business. Instead, I have called you friends, for everything that I learned from my Father I have made known to you."
John 15:15

I am *Protected*

"But the Lord is faithful, and he will strengthen you and protect you from the evil one."
2 Thessalonians 3:3

I am *FEARFULLY* & *WONDERFULLY* made

"I praise you because I am fearfully and wonderfully made; your works are wonderful, I know that full well."
Psalm 139:14

I am GOD'S *Masterpiece*

"For we are God's masterpiece. He has created us anew in Christ Jesus, so we can do the good things He planned for us long ago."
Ephesians 2:10

"But you are a chosen people, a royal priesthood, a holy nation, God's special possession, that you may declare the praises of him who called you out of darkness into his wonderful light."
1 peter 2:9

Remember who **God** says you are

I am FEARFULLY & WONDERFULLY

Masterpiece Confident

Valuable

Loved

Protected

Friend

Chosen

THE DAUGHTER OF A *KING* Blessed

and so much more...

www.ingramcontent.com/pod-product-compliance
Lightning Source LLC
Chambersburg PA
CBHW041408160426
42811CB00103B/1554